D0516499

ADVENTURES

Rocket to the Moon

by Wendy Clemson
and David Clemson

Math and curriculum
consultant: Debra Voege, M.A.,
science and math curriculum
resource teacher

GARETH**STEVENS**
GS
PUBLISHING
A Member of the WRC Media Family of Companies

Please visit our Web site at: www.garethstevens.com
For a free color catalog describing Gareth Stevens
Publishing's list of high-quality books and multimedia
programs, call 1-800-542-2595 (USA)
or 1-800-387-3178 (Canada).
Gareth Stevens Publishing's fax: (414) 332-3567

Library of Congress Cataloging-in-Publication
Data available upon request from publisher.
Fax (414) 336-0157 for the attention of the
Publishing Records Department.

ISBN-13: 978-0-8368-7841-7 (lib. bdg.)
ISBN-13: 978-0-8368-8140-0 (softcover)

This North American edition first published in 2007 by
Gareth Stevens Publishing
A Member of the WRC Media Family of Companies
330 West Olive Street, Suite 100
Milwaukee, WI 53212 USA

ticktock project editor: Rebecca Clunes
ticktock project designer: Sara Greasley
Gareth Stevens editor: Tea Benduhn
Gareth Stevens art direction: Tammy West
Gareth Stevens graphic designer: Kami Strunsee
Gareth Stevens production: Jessica Yanke and Robert Kraus

Picture credits
t=top, b=bottom, c=center, l=left, r=right
Christian Deforeit 15; ESA/D. Ducros 32; ESA/J. Huart 6l; Jerry Mason/Science Photo Library 19; NASA 5, 8, 10,
16b, 16t, 17t, 22, 23, 24b, 24t, 25, 26, 29t, 29b; Science Photo Library/NASA 17b, 27; Shutterstock 1, 4 (all),
9b, 11, 12-13 (all), 31t, 31b; Ticktock Media archive 2, 6-7, 9t, 20t, 21tl, 21tr, 28, 30; Detlev van Ravenswaay/
Science Photo Library 20-21.

Printed in Canada

1 2 3 4 5 6 7 8 9 10 10 09 08 07 06

CONTENTS

MEASUREMENT CONVERSIONS

1 inch = 2.5 centimeters
1 foot = 0.3 meter
1 mile = 1.6 kilometers
1 ounce = 28.3 grams
1 pound = 0.5 kilogram

1 cup = 240 milliliters
1 pint = 0.5 liter
1 quart = 1 liter
1 gallon = 3.8 liters

To change from Fahrenheit (F) to Celsius (C):
Fahrenheit (F)° − 32° ÷ 1.8 = Celsius (C)°

WELCOME TO SPACE

You have an amazing job. You are an astronaut! Soon, you will be taking your first trip into space. When your rocket is in space, you will feel weightless, and you will be able to float around. You will also be able to see planet Earth from the window!

Going into space is an exciting and important job.

Astronauts are scientists who do important research.

Anyone who goes into space must be very healthy.

Some astronauts are great pilots. They fly rockets and airplanes.

In space, astronauts live in a small area, so they have to know how to get along with other people.

Did you know that astronauts need to use math?

Inside this book, you will find math puzzles that astronauts have to solve every day. You will also have a chance to answer number questions about your adventure in space.

What is inside the book?

Charts and tables will help you answer the math questions.

Find out what needs to be done next in your busy day.

Answer the questions and practice your math skills.

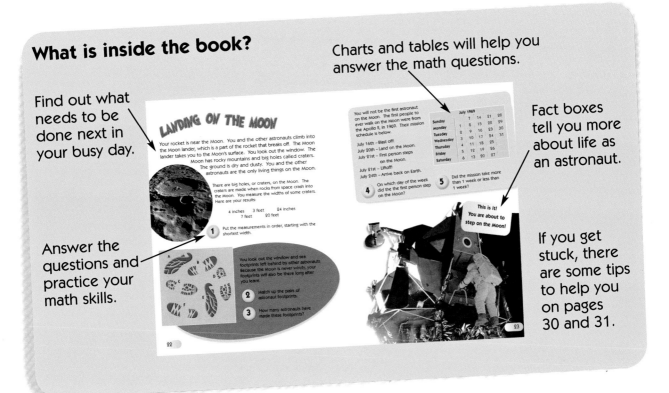

Fact boxes tell you more about life as an astronaut.

If you get stuck, there are some tips to help you on pages 30 and 31.

Are you ready to be an astronaut for the day?

You will need paper, a pencil, and a ruler, and don't forget to wear your space suit. Let's go!

HEADING TO THE MOON

You have been chosen to take part in a space mission. Your rocket will blast off into space and travel 239,000 miles to the Moon. Your mission will take about one week. Let's find out about the Moon!

Have you noticed that the Moon looks full, or like a circle, some days of the month? Other days, it is just a sliver. To go from one full Moon to the next full Moon takes 29 days. This amount of time is called a lunar month.

 1 How many days are in 2 lunar months?

 2 Is 29 an odd number or an even number?

THE SHAPE OF THE MOON

The Moon seems to change its shape during the lunar month. Some of the Moon shapes we see are pictured below.

A   B   C   D   E

 3 Which of the shapes above is a circle?

 4 What is the shape of Moon C?

Moon

Earth

The Moon is about 4 times smaller than Earth.

A journey from Earth to the Moon is the same distance as driving around Earth about 10 times! Answer the times ten (x 10) questions below.

5 Every day, you run 3 miles. How many miles would you go if you ran 10 times as far?

6 You love to drink milk. Every day, you drink ½ pint of milk. How much milk would you drink if you drank 10 times as much?

7 You have a pet mouse. Imagine if your mouse were 10 times as big! Would your mouse be the size of
A a guinea pig?   B a cat?   C an elephant?

ASTRONAUT TRAINING

Learning how to be an astronaut takes a long time. Your training is a lot of work, but it is fun. You learn how to fly a rocket, how to breathe in your space suit, and how to walk in space. You also make friends with the other people training to be astronauts.

ASTRONAUT CHART

name	Sam	Tasha	José
age	19 years	22 years	25 years
height	6 feet	5 feet	6 feet 6 inches

1 You start training with Sam, Tasha, and José. The training actually takes 10 years before an astronaut goes into space. If they train for 10 years, how old will Sam, Tasha, and José be when they go into space?

2 The first rockets ever made were very small. Only short people were able to fit inside them. Which of the astronauts above would fit best inside a small rocket?

3 An astronaut wears a special suit in space. Space suits weigh about 22 pounds. 22 is between 20 and 30. What other whole numbers are between 20 and 30?

FLIGHT TRAINING

As part of your training, you have to learn how to fly a jet.
To fly a jet, you need to be able to steer it.

 4 The fighter plane below has made a ¼ turn clockwise. Which of the planes to the right have also made a ¼ turn?

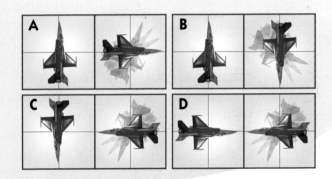

There is no air in space. When astronauts go outside the rocket, they wear a space suit that gives them oxygen to breathe.

THE SPACE ROCKET

You have finished your training, and you are ready to go to the Moon. The space rocket is ready, too! The rocket will be your home for the next week.

The bottom of the rocket has five pipes. The pipes are arranged in a pattern that looks like the pattern to the right.

1 Which of the rockets below has its pipes arranged in the same pattern as your rocket?

A   B   C   D

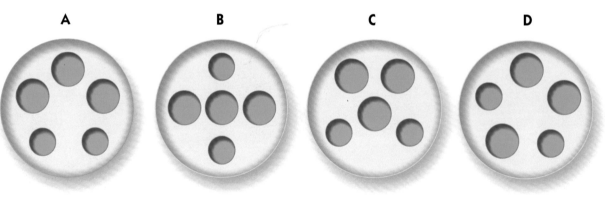

2 A rocket can sit on a launch pad for many weeks. The clock to the right shows how many hours, minutes, and seconds until the rocket launches. Is the number shown

   A about 1 week?
   B about 4 days?
   C about 3 days?
   D about 2 days?

This shape is on the tower.

3 How many sides does this shape have?

4 How many corners does this shape have?

The rocket's engines are at the bottom of the rocket. The astronauts sit near the top of the rocket.

5 The shapes below are on the rocket. What is the name of each shape?

A

B

Your rocket is ready to blast off into space!

WE HAVE LIFTOFF!

This is it! You say goodbye to your family and friends as you board the rocket. You do the final checks, and then you strap yourself into your seat. The rocket starts to shake. BOOM! You have liftoff!

At 10:00 a.m., the astronauts load fuel into the space rocket. Then, 3 hours later, you board the space rocket. You take 2 hours to do the final checks, and 1 hour after that, the rocket launches into space!

1 At what time does the rocket launch?

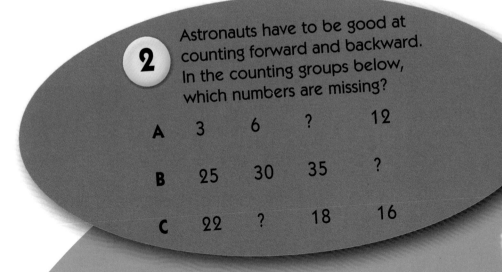

2 Astronauts have to be good at counting forward and backward. In the counting groups below, which numbers are missing?

A   3   6   ?   12

B   25   30   35   ?

C   22   ?   18   16

After liftoff, parts of the rocket fall away. The rocket is now lighter, so it can go faster. The number line in the box below shows when each part falls off.

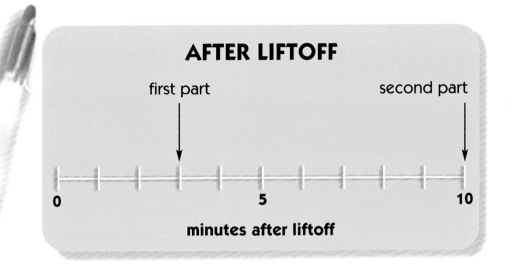

AFTER LIFTOFF

first part   second part

0   5   10

minutes after liftoff

3 How many minutes after liftoff does the first part of the rocket fall away?

4 How many minutes after liftoff does the second part fall away?

Missions to the Moon have three astronauts, but only two of them get to walk on the Moon. For safety reasons, one person has to stay in the rocket.

THE STARS IN SPACE

Your space rocket has a window, and whenever you can, you look out at the stars. Wow! There are so many of them! They seem much brighter in space. A pattern of stars is called a constellation. There are 88 constellations in the sky.

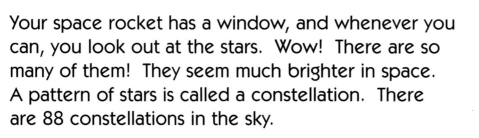

The number track below is for counting constellations.

77		79	80							87	88

1 Which of these numbers would NOT go into this number track?
71   85   76   89   86   84

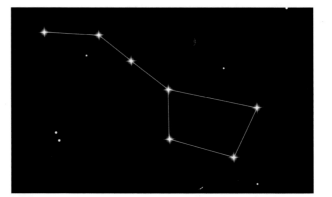

2 The group of stars to the right is called the Big Dipper. How many stars make up this constellation?

3 How many line segments join the stars in the Big Dipper?

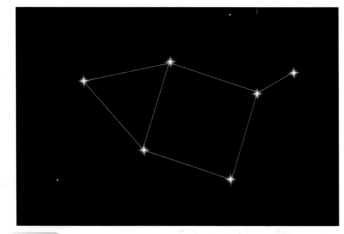

4 The group of stars to the left is another constellation. How many stars make the triangle?

5 How many stars make the rectangle?

There are 7 main types of stars. One of the biggest types of stars is the red supergiant, which is much bigger than the Sun. A white dwarf is one of the smallest. You will have to count stars on your trip. Try this star math.

6 11 red supergiants plus 8 red supergiants

8 9 white dwarfs added to 17 white dwarfs

7 14 red supergiants take away 13 red supergiants

9 30 white dwarfs minus 22 white dwarfs

We can see stars much better in space. Earth's atmosphere makes it hard to see the night sky clearly.

LIFE IN SPACE

It takes a few days to get used to living in space. Floating around the rocket as if you do not weigh anything feels unusual. Common activities, such as eating, drinking, and sleeping, are hard to do in space. You cannot wash your clothes in space, either, so you wear them for three days and then throw them away.

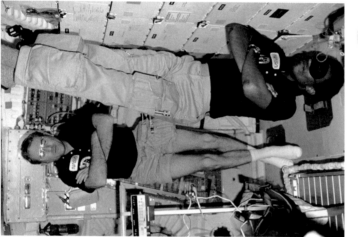

1 Astronauts do not all sleep at the same time. You sleep for 4 hours, then you are awake for 8 hours. You repeat this pattern throughout the day. How many times will you sleep in 24 hours?

ASTRONAUT FOOD

breakfast	lunch	dinner
cereal	tortilla	beans
raisins	chicken	rice
pear	peanuts	mixed fruit
orange juice	apple juice	tea

A lot of astronaut food comes in packets so the food will not float around the rocket.

2 Look at the menu in the table to the left. For which meal will you eat rice?

3 What do you drink at breakfast?

Water must not be wasted in space. Astronauts have a special shower that uses very little water.

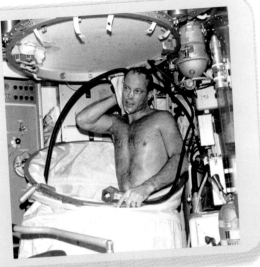

 4 A space shower uses about 1 gallon of water. How many cups is that?

5 Each astronaut uses about 2½ gallons of water each day. How many quarts is that?

Astronauts need the same vitamins in space that they need on Earth. Fresh fruit helps them stay healthy.

BACK AT MISSION CONTROL

Back on Earth, lots of people are in the mission control room. They make sure the space rocket is working properly, and the astronauts are healthy. They use computers linked to the rocket to get their information.

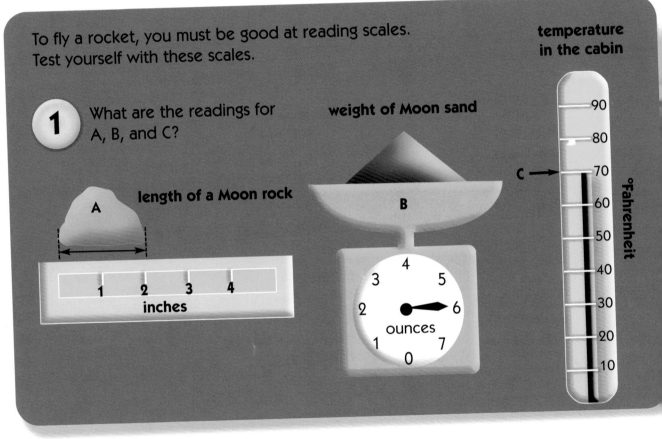

To fly a rocket, you must be good at reading scales. Test yourself with these scales.

temperature in the cabin

1 What are the readings for A, B, and C?

weight of Moon sand

length of a Moon rock

A

1 2 3 4
inches

B

4
3   5
2   6
ounces
1   7
0

C →

90
80
70
60
50
40
30
20
10

°Fahrenheit

The computers at mission control have red and green lights on them. The green lights mean everything is working. A red light means something is wrong. Look at the pattern of lights below.

2 What color is the second light?

3 What color is the sixth light?

In space, you feel weightless. You can float inside the rocket.

This food bar can float, too. On Earth, it weighs 2 ounces.

4 How much in total do these bars weigh on Earth?

5 How much in total do these bars weigh on Earth?

6 Mission control needs to make sure that you are not too tired and that your brain is sharp. Below is a thinking puzzle for you. What is the mystery number?

| mystery number | – | 4 | = | 8 |

EARTH'S SOLAR SYSTEM

Earth's solar system has eight known planets. Earth is one of the planets. Astronauts want to know about the other planets, too. If your journey to the Moon goes well, you might be asked to take part in a mission to the planet Mars.

Look at the picture at the bottom of these pages.
It shows the Sun and all of the planets in the solar system.

1 Which planets are closer to the Sun than Earth?

2 Is Mars bigger than Earth?

3 Which is bigger — Earth or Neptune?

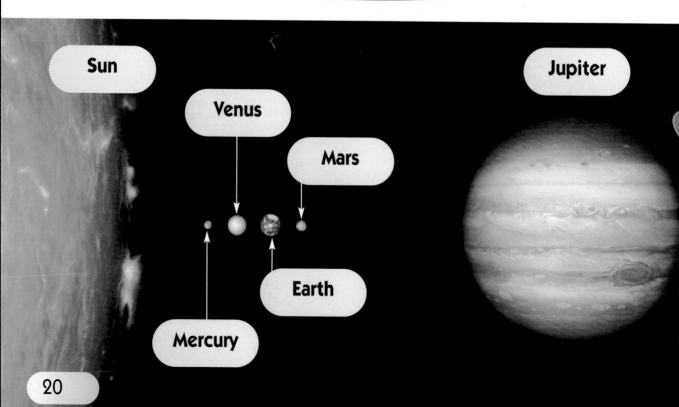

Sun

Jupiter

Venus

Mars

Earth

Mercury

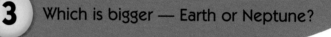

The planets closest to Earth are Venus and Mars.

4 Which of the planets to the right is called the Red Planet?

5 Which of the planets to the right has 2 moons?

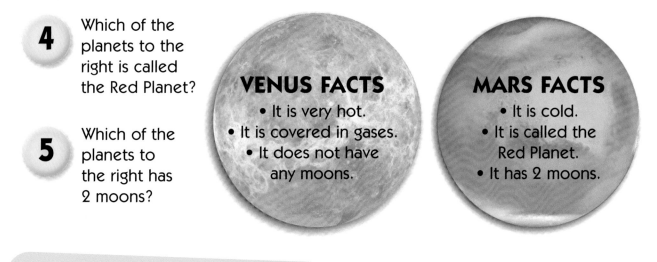

VENUS FACTS
- It is very hot.
- It is covered in gases.
- It does not have any moons.

MARS FACTS
- It is cold.
- It is called the Red Planet.
- It has 2 moons.

6 Neptune, Jupiter, and Uranus have lots of moons. One of these three planets has 15 moons, one has 8 moons, and one has 16 moons. You know that
- Jupiter has the most moons.
- Neptune has the least moons.

A How many moons does Neptune have?
B How many moons does Jupiter have?
C How many moons does Uranus have?

Saturn

Uranus

Neptune

LANDING ON THE MOON

Your rocket is near the Moon. You and the other astronauts climb into the Moon lander, which is a part of the rocket that breaks off. The Moon lander takes you to the Moon's surface. You look out the window. The Moon has rocky mountains and big holes called craters. The ground is dry and dusty. You and the other astronauts are the only living things on the Moon.

There are big holes, or craters, on the Moon. The craters were made when rocks from space crashed into the Moon. You measure the widths of some craters. Here are your results:

4 inches	3 feet	24 inches
	7 feet	20 feet

1 Put the measurements in order, starting with the shortest width.

You look out the window and see footprints left behind by other astronauts. Because the Moon is never windy, your footprints will also be there long after you leave.

2 Match up the pairs of astronaut footprints.

3 How many astronauts have made these footprints?

The first people ever to walk on the Moon were from *Apollo 11*, in 1969. Their mission schedule is shown below. Use the calendar to the right to help you answer the questions about the *Apollo 11* mission.

July 16 – blast off

July 20 – land on the Moon

July 21 – First person steps on the Moon.

July 21 – leave the Moon

July 24 – arrive back on Earth

July 1969					
Sunday		7	14	21	28
Monday	1	8	15	22	29
Tuesday	2	9	16	23	30
Wednesday	3	10	17	24	31
Thursday	4	11	18	25	
Friday	5	12	19	26	
Saturday	6	13	20	27	

 4 On which day of the week did the first person step on the Moon?

5 Did the mission take more than 1 week or less than 1 week?

> This is it! You are about to step onto the Moon!

WALKING ON THE MOON

The door of your Moon lander opens slowly. You walk down the steps and then stand on the Moon. You are finally here! Walking on the Moon is fun. You weigh much less here than you do on Earth so walking is more like bouncing.

FINDING YOUR WAY

The grid map to the right shows part of the Moon.

Moon lander   **crater**   **small rock**   **large rock**

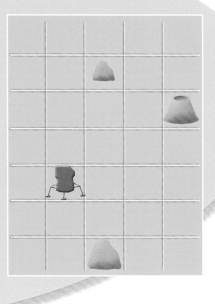

1 From the Moon lander, the small rock is 1 square right and 3 squares up. What are the directions from the Moon lander to the crater?

2 How would you reach the large rock from the Moon lander?

3 You have been asked to collect some rocks from the Moon. Back on Earth, scientists will study the rocks to find out more about the Moon. You collect 44 pounds of Moon rocks. How many boxes will you need if each box can carry 4 pounds of Moon rocks?

4 How many boxes will you need if each box can carry 5 pounds?

Neil Armstrong and Buzz Aldrin were the first people to stand on the Moon.

BIGGEST AND HEAVIEST

You collect rocks and put them in boxes. The biggest boxes are not always the heaviest. You use a balance to weigh the boxes to the right.

5 Which of the pink boxes is heavier?

6 Which of the yellow boxes is lighter?

7 Which of the blue boxes is heavier?

A

B

A

B

B

A

RETURNING TO EARTH

Your rocket is carrying a capsule. When you get close to Earth, you and the other astronauts climb into the capsule. The capsule breaks away from the rocket and brings you back to Earth. You splash down safely into the sea. Your mission has been a success.

1 The capsule goes very fast. Put the items below in order from the fastest to the slowest:
running cheetah = 70 miles per hour
rocket capsule = 24,000 miles per hour
high-speed train = 260 miles per hour

2 The capsule has three parachutes to slow it down. One parachute has 20 strings. What number needs to be added in each of the following math puzzles to make 20?

$19 + ? = 20$ $7 + ? = 20$
$3 + ? = 20$ $16 + ? = 20$

SPLASH DOWN IN THE SEA

Your capsule lands in the sea. Rescue crews arrive on planes, ships, and helicopters to pick up all the astronauts.

type of pick-up vehicle

planes

ships

helicopters

1   2   3   4   5   6
number of pick-up vehicles

3 How many helicopters arrive?

4 How many vehicles arrive in total?

Your capsule splashes into the water. You have made a safe landing.

YOU ARE HOME!

Your capsule lands in the sea at 2:00 p.m. The table to the right shows the times that you and the other astronauts actually step out of the capsule.

José	2:11 p.m.
Tasha	2:06 p.m.
you	2:13 p.m.
Sam	2:09 p.m.

5 Who is first out of the capsule?

6 How many minutes after landing is everyone out of the capsule?

BACK HOME

You have landed safely back on Earth. Your trip to the Moon has been amazing. Of course, everybody wants to hear about your journey. Newspaper and television reporters crowd around you, wanting to hear your story. You are famous!

After your capsule lands in the sea, you have a few more tasks to complete. To answer the questions below, figure out the answers to the number puzzles that follow each question.

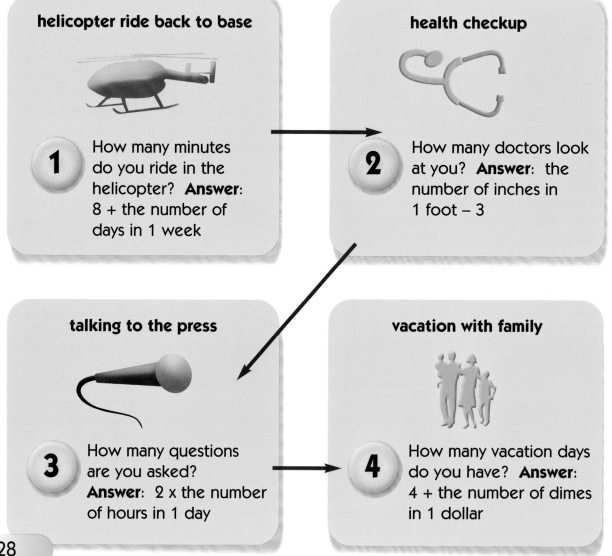

helicopter ride back to base

1 How many minutes do you ride in the helicopter? **Answer:** 8 + the number of days in 1 week

health checkup

2 How many doctors look at you? **Answer:** the number of inches in 1 foot − 3

talking to the press

3 How many questions are you asked? **Answer:** 2 x the number of hours in 1 day

vacation with family

4 How many vacation days do you have? **Answer:** 4 + the number of dimes in 1 dollar

5 Each space mission has its own badge. The badge to the right is the *Apollo 11* badge. Your mission's badge is one of the three badges below.
- It has two circles to show Earth and the Moon.
- It has a triangle to represent the space rocket.
- It has a square to represent the 4 astronauts on your team.

Which is your badge?

A   B   C

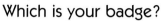

Your mission is over. It is time for the next team to go into space. Well done, astronaut!

TIPS AND HELP

PAGES 6-7

Odds and evens - Even numbers are in the pattern of counting by twos: 2, 4, 6, 8, 10, and so on. Odd numbers are all numbers that are not even: 1, 3, 5, 7, 9, and so on.

PAGES 8-9

Adding ten - When you add ten to a number, you need to increase the tens in that number by 1 ten. For example, 19 has 1 ten (and 9 ones). If we add 1 ten, we make 2 tens, and the answer is 29 (2 tens and 9 ones).

A ¼ turn - There are 4 quarter turns in 1 complete turn.

Clockwise - is the direction the hands of a clock move.

clockwise

PAGES 10-11

Number of hours in a day - There are 24 hours in one day, 48 hours in two days, 72 hours in three days, and 96 hours in four days.

Shapes - Remember these shapes:

 Cylinder: The two faces at the ends of a cylinder are circles.

 Cone: The flat base of a cone is a circle.

PAGES 12-13

Telling time - The shorter hand on a clock is the hour hand. It shows us what hour (or "o'clock") it is. If you move the hour hand forward 3 hours, then 2 hours, and then 1 hour, the hour hand's new position will show the launch time.

Number line - The number line here is measuring minutes. Each mark on the line means 1 minute.

PAGES 14-15

Adding up - The words "plus," "add up," "add to," and "sum" all mean the same. You can add numbers in any order. It can be easier to add 10, so if you find 11 or 9 in a sum, you could add 10 and then take away or add 1 to get the answer. For example:
11 + 8 gives the same answer as 10 + 8 + 1
9 + 17 gives the same answer as 10 + 17 − 1

Taking away - "Take away," "minus," and "subtract" all mean the same.

PAGES 16-17

Day - There are 24 hours in 1 day. A day starts at midnight and lasts until the next midnight.

Measurements - There are 4 cups in 1 quart. There are 4 quarts in 1 gallon.

PAGES 18-19

Scales - In math, scales help us see measurements. Check the scale to see what type of measurement is shown. For example, a ruler measures inches.

Counting by twos - Count out loud: 2, 4, 6, 8, 10, 12, 14, 16, 18, 20. Remembering this pattern is useful.

PAGES 20-21

Comparing things - When we compare the sizes of two things, we say one is "bigger than" the other. When we compare the sizes of three or more things, we say that one of them is "biggest." When we compare two numbers, we use the words "more" or "less." When we compare three or more numbers, we use the words "most" or "least."

PAGES 22-23

Putting measurements in order - First, check that all the measurements use the same unit of measurement. (Here, the units are inches and feet.) If the units of measurement are not the same, change them all to the same unit. Next, look for the smallest number. The smallest whole numbers have no tens (only ones, or units). They are the numbers 1, 2, 3, 4, 5, 6, 7, 8, and 9. Then, look for numbers with only 1 ten (such as 12) and put the number with the fewest units first, followed by the others, in order. Now see if any numbers have more than 1 ten and put those in order of the number of tens they have. Continue until you have arranged all of the numbers.

Calendar - A calendar shows the day of the week for each date in a month. We can read a calendar from top to bottom or from left to right. On this calendar, the days of the week go from top to bottom along the side. Each row across, from left to right, shows the dates for each day of the week.

PAGES 24-25

Grid maps - You find the path for objects on a grid map by moving right or left, then up or down (or up or down, then right or left).

Grouping - When we break up a number into equal parts, each part forms a group, or a fraction of the whole. Making groups is called dividing.

PAGES 26-27

Making 20 - It is useful to know the pairs of numbers that add up to 20. Continue the following pattern:
  0 + 20
  1 + 19
  2 + 18 . . .

Bar graph - A bar graph compares two types of information. In this bar graph, one colored box means one vehicle, and the graph compares numbers of types of vehicle.

Time - Time is shown as an hour followed by minutes. For example, 8:27 a.m. means the time is 27 minutes past the hour of 8 in the morning.

PAGES 28-29

Equal measures - There are
• 7 days in 1 week
• 12 inches in 1 foot
• 24 hours in 1 day
• 10 dimes in 1 dollar

ANSWERS

PAGES 6-7

1 58 days
2 odd number
3 E
4 half circle or semicircle
5 30 miles
6 5 pints
7 B a cat

PAGES 8-9

1 Sam = 29 years old
   Tasha = 32 years old
   José = 35 years old
2 Tasha
3 21, 23, 24, 25, 26, 27, 28, and 29
4 A and C

PAGES 10-11

1 D
2 about 3 days
3 4 sides
4 4 corners
5 A = cylinder
   B = cone

PAGES 12-13

1 4:00 p.m.
2 A = 9
   B = 40
   C = 20
3 3 minutes
4 10 minutes

PAGES 14-15

1 71, 76, and 89
2 7 stars
3 7 line segments
4 3 stars
5 4 stars
6 19 red supergiants
7 1 red supergiant
8 26 white dwarfs
9 8 white dwarfs

PAGES 16-17

1 2 times
2 dinner
3 orange juice
4 16 cups
5 10 quarts

PAGES 18-19

1 A = 2 inches
   B = 6 ounces
   C = 70 °F
2 green
3 green
4 4 ounces
5 10 ounces
6 12

PAGES 20-21

1 Mercury and Venus
2 no
3 Neptune
4 Mars
5 Mars
6 A = 8 moons
   B = 16 moons
   C = 15 moons

PAGES 22-23

1 4 inches, 24 inches, 3 feet, 7 feet, and 20 feet
2 A and E
   B and F
   C and D
3 3 astronauts
4 Sunday
5 more than 1 week

PAGES 24-25

1 3 squares right and 2 squares up
2 1 square right and 2 squares down
3 11 boxes
4 9 boxes
5 box B
6 box A
7 box A

PAGES 26-27

1 rocket capsule
   high-speed train
   running cheetah
2 19 + 1, 7 + 13, 3 + 17, 16 + 4
3 6 helicopters
4 14 vehicles
5 Tasha
6 13 minutes

PAGES 28-29

1 15 minutes
2 9 doctors
3 48 questions
4 14 vacation days
5 C